THE MANNERS BOOK

What's Right, Ned?

By June Behrens

Photographs by Michele and Tom Grimm

A Golden Gate Junior Book   Childrens Press · Chicago

To Jackie Tripp

The photographers wish to thank Chris Becker and the other boys and girls at Palisades School in Capistrano Beach, California, for their generous help in making possible the photographs in this book.

Library of Congress Cataloging in Publication Data

Behrens, June.
  The manners book.

  "A Golden Gate junior book."
  SUMMARY: Chris' stuffed bear Ned answers questions about the proper thing to do in a number of social situations.
  1. Etiquette for children and youth. [1. Etiquette] I. Grimm, Michele. II. Grimm, Tom. III. Title.
BJ1857.C5B384   395′.1′22   79-22377
ISBN 0-516-08750-9

THE MANNERS BOOK touches on aspects of positive behavior—*please, thank you, excuse me, you're welcome, I'm sorry,* as well as *introductions, table manners, helping, sharing.* Chris and his stuffed bear Ned meet daily life situations and solve the problem of the correct response.

Miss Davis said, "Who spilled the paint?"

The bottle turned over on the floor.

What should I do, Ned?

I'd say, "It was an accident.

I did it and I'm sorry."

Aunt Michele brought me a present.

It was for my birthday.

What should I say, Ned?

I'd say, "Thank you, Aunt Michele.

I like presents!"

I was eating jellybeans.

Veronica came over to play with me.

What would you do, Ned?

I'd say, "Would you like

a jellybean, Veronica?"

I gave Edwardo my favorite marble.

He said, "Thank you!"

Should I say anything, Ned?

I'd say, "You're welcome,

Edwardo."

11

We had a picnic in the park.

I needed something for my sandwich.

Should I reach way over, Ned?

I'd say, "Please pass

the mustard."

I bumped a boy at school.

He fell down and I helped him up.

What would you say, Ned?

I'd say, "Excuse me. I didn't

mean to bump you. It was an accident."

Tien asked me a question at lunch.

My mouth was full of food.

What would you do, Ned?

"I'd talk after I swallowed my food."

Hilda and Maria were talking.

I had something important to say.

What should I do, Ned?

"I'd wait my turn to talk."

Ralph brought his father to school.

He wanted to meet me.

What's the right thing to say, Ned?

I'd say, "How do you do,

Mr. Cooper."

I called Wayne on the phone.

His mother answered.

What would you say, Ned?

I'd say, "Hello, my name is Ned.

May I please speak to Wayne?"

Keith just moved next door.

He wanted a friend.

What would you do, Ned?

I'd say, "My name is Ned.

Will you play with me?"

25

I took Keith home with me.

Mom was in the kitchen.

What's the right thing to say, Ned?

I'd say, "Mother, meet my

friend Keith."

Katie was a new girl at school.

She looked lost.

What's right to do, Ned?

I'd say, "Let me help you, Katie.

We will find the teacher."

Ned, you know all the answers.

Thanks for helping me.

Thinking of others is just good manners.

I feel good when I know what's right.

For most young children, learning manners—what to say, what to do, how to behave in an unexpected or unaccustomed situation—can be an exceedingly troublesome matter. In this book, June Behrens, a specialist in early childhood education with years of experience in teaching the very young (she is also a parent as well as a teacher), presents a delightfully different approach to the problem through a series of common everyday experiences encountered by a little boy and his beloved stuffed bear. Charming full-page color photographs of Chris, his toy companion, and the many children he comes in contact with as he meets a wide variety of situations, will please as well as instruct primary age readers.

June Behrens has covered an exceedingly wide range of subjects in her many successful books for young readers. A gifted teacher, she was a reading specialist in one of California's largest public school systems for many years. A native Californian, she is a graduate of the University of California at Santa Barbara. She has a Master's degree in Administration from the University of Southern California and holds a Credential in Early Childhood Education. Among her many popular titles, published by Childrens Press, are, *Twisters, Desert Animals, Canal Boats West, Lighthouse Family, Looking At Beasties, Whalewatch!* and *My Name Is Jimmy Carter.* She is the author of several plays for children, most recently a play about Martin Luther King, Jr.

Michele and Tom Grimm are well known as a writer-photographer team with many bylines to their credit. Their work has appeared in a wide variety of national publications, including Scholastic's *Dynamite* and *Bananas* magazines. The couple writes a weekly travel column for the *Los Angeles Times*, and a bimonthly photography column for *Travel/Holiday* magazine. They are the authors and illustrators of *All About 35mm Photography,* published by Macmillan, *Florida,* published by Kodansha/Harper & Row, *The Basic Book of Photography* and *The Basic Darkroom Book,* published by the New American Library. They have also done photographic illustrations for a number of children's books, including June Behren's *What I Hear* and *What is a Seal?* The Grimms live in Laguna Beach, a seaside community in Southern California.